How to Eat Pizza

1. Read   2. Cut   3. Paste in order

	1
	2
	3
	4

Bite into the pizza.

Lick your lips!

Pick up the biggest part.

Cut the pizza into parts.

What do you like on your pizza?

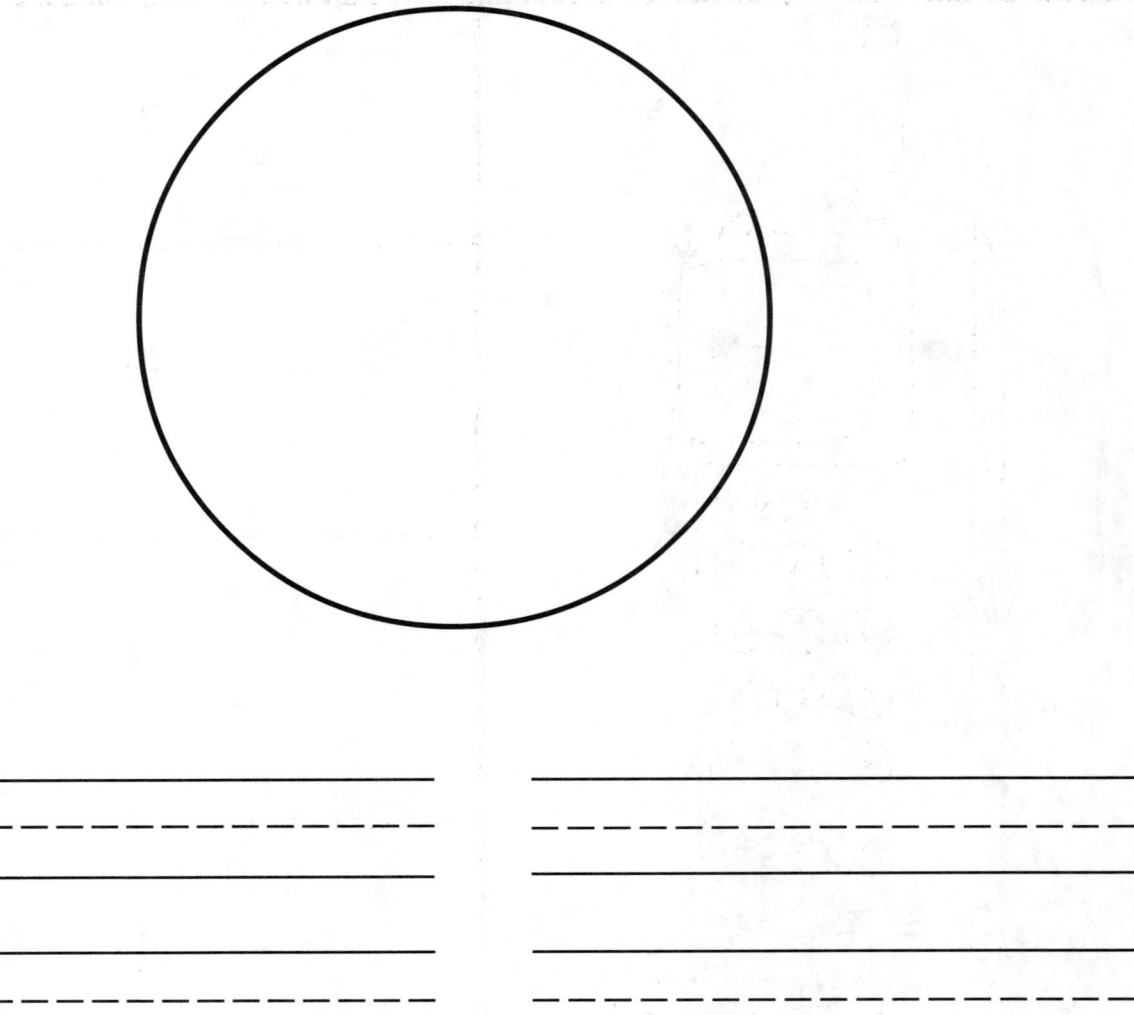

How to Use a Telephone

1. Read 2. Cut 3. Paste in order

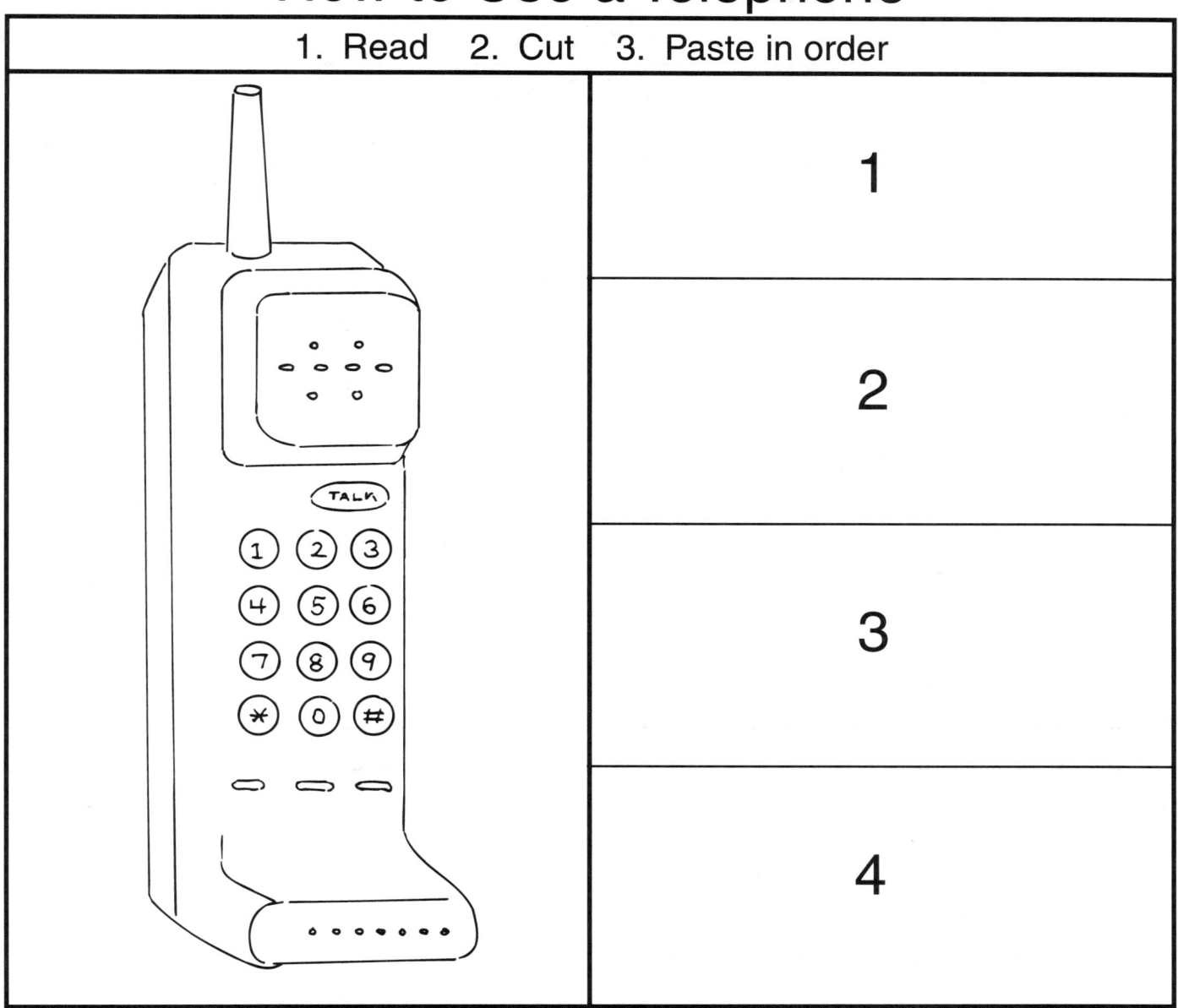

| 1 |
| 2 |
| 3 |
| 4 |

Talk to your friend.

Hang up the telephone.

Pick up the telephone.

Call the number you want.

I call these people: Telephone Number:

How to Feed the Cat

1. Read   2. Cut   3. Paste in order

	1
	2
	3
	4

Take the lid off the can.

Call your cat.

Put the cat food in the dish.

Get a can of cat food and a dish.

This is my pet. Its name is _____

_____

How I take care of my pet:
_____
_____
_____
_____

How to Make a Mask

1. Read   2. Cut   3. Paste in order

	1
	2
	3
	4

Put on the mask and surprise your pal.

Get a big brown bag.

Cut out two eyes so you can see.

Now draw a nose and a mouth.

Make a Mask

You need: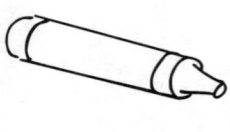

1. Put the bag on your head. Make an X with a crayon where your eyes are.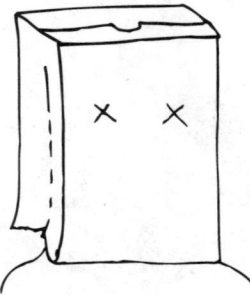

2. Take bag off your head. Cut out where the X is for eye holes.

3. Draw a face on your mask.

How to Put on a Jacket

1. Read   2. Cut   3. Paste in order

	1
	2
	3
	4

Put your arms in the sleeves.

Zip up your jacket.

It is a cold day. Get your jacket.

Now you can go out to play.

Draw a picture of your jacket.

What does your jacket have?

buttons   snaps   zipper

How to Eat a Cookie

1. Read 2. Cut 3. Paste in order

	1
	2
	3
	4

Take big bites and eat them up.

Take your cookies outside and sit on the back step.

Lick the last bits off your fingers.

Take two cookies out of the box.

Draw the cookie you like best on this plate.

Why do you like this cookie best?

How to Ride a Bike

1. Read   2. Cut   3. Paste in order

	1
	2
	3
	4

- Push the pedals so you can go down the street.
- Put on the brakes to stop.
- Put your hands on the handle bars and get on the bike.
- Put your feet on the pedals.

A bike is fun to ride.
Draw something else you like to ride.

I like to ride _____ .
Tell why you like to ride it.

_____
_____
_____
_____

How to Make an Ice Cream Cone

1. Read   2. Cut   3. Paste in order

	1
	2
	3
	4

Take a big lick and gobble it down.

Then get the ice cream from the freezer.

First get a scoop and a cone.

Take a big scoop of ice cream and put it on the cone.

Fill this ice cream cone.

How many scoops do you have?

What flavors do you have?

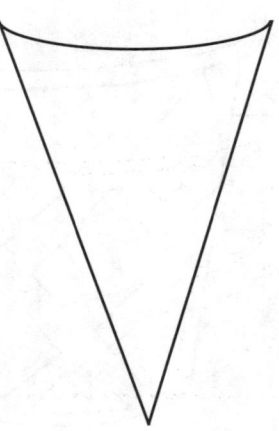

How to Clean Your Dog

1. Read   2. Cut   3. Paste in order

	1
	2
	3
	4
	5
	6

Put him in the water.

Wash the suds off the dog.

Dry him with the big towel and let him go.

Now catch your dog.

Fill your tub with water and get a big towel.

Rub the suds all over your dog.

How do you think the dog got dirty?

Draw the clean dog here.

How to Catch a Tadpole

1. Read   2. Cut   3. Paste in order

	1
	2
	3
	4
	5
	6

Put holes in the lid.	Look in the water until you see tadpoles.
Put the lid on the jar and take them home.	Find a jar at your house.
Go to a pond.	Scoop up some tadpoles in your jar.

The little tadpoles will grow up to be frogs.

Draw a big frog sitting on a log.
Make the log in a pond.

How to Pick an Apple

1. Read   2. Cut   3. Paste in order

	1
	2
	3
	4
	5
	6

Get a bag and a ladder.	Take the bag of apples in the house.
Pick the apples and put them in the bag.	Go down the ladder.
Go up the ladder.	Put the ladder by the tree.

 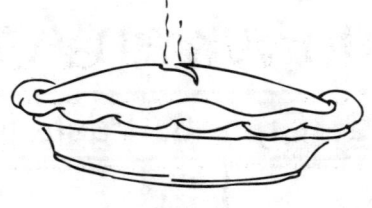 

apple apple pie apple jelly

Apples taste good.
We can eat apples.
We can put apples in a pie.
We can make jelly from apples.

Draw the way you like apples best.

How to Wrap a Gift

1. Read   2. Cut   3. Paste in order

1	
2	
3	
4	
5	
6	

Wrap the box in pretty paper.

Set the gift in a box.

Now put on the lid.

Tape a ribbon on the box.

Stick a card under the ribbon.

Take the gift to the party.

Draw what is in the box.

Who would you give the gift to? _____

How to Take a Bath

1. Read   2. Cut   3. Paste in order

	1
	2
	3
	4
	5
	6

Add bubble bath.	Get dressed.
Get out of the tub and dry off.	Get into the tub.
Fill the tub with water.	Wash with soap and a rag.

Why do you have to take baths?

_____

_____

_____
_____

_____

Do you like a bath or a shower best? _____

Do you like bubble bath in your tub? _____

Station 5: Sequencing

How to Make a Sandwich

1. Read   2. Cut   3. Paste in order

	1
	2
	3
	4
	5
	6

Cut the sandwich in two.	Open the jar of peanut butter.
Eat it up!	Get out the bread, peanut butter, and a knife.
Sit down and take a big bite.	Put a lot of peanut butter on the bread.

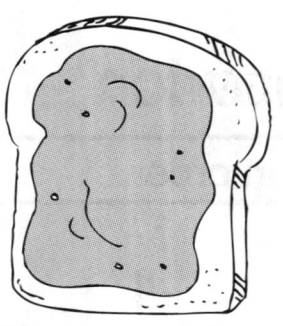 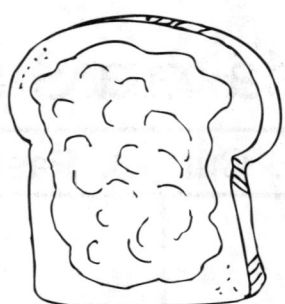

Do you like peanut butter and jelly sandwiches? _____

What kind of sandwich do you like best?
_____
_____

How do you make it?
_____
_____
_____
_____
_____

How to Plant a Seed

1. Read   2. Cut   3. Paste in order

	1
	2
	3
	4
	5
	6

Water the seeds.

Pick out the seeds you want to plant.

Fill the hole with dirt and pat it down.

Now the seeds can grow.

Next you must dig a hole in the dirt.

Drop the seeds into the hole.

Draw what you think will grow from the seeds in the pot.

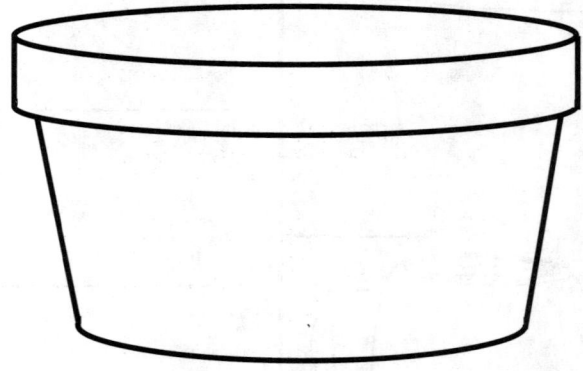

Answer Key

Please take time to go over the work your child has completed. Ask your child to explain what he/she has done. Praise both success and effort. If mistakes have been made, explain what the answer should have been and how to find it. Let your child know that mistakes are a part of learning. The time you spend with your child helps let him/her know you feel learning is important.

page 1

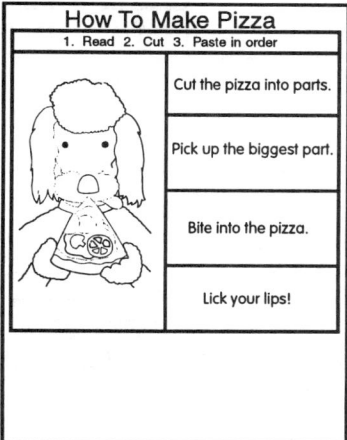

How To Make Pizza
1. Read 2. Cut 3. Paste in order

- Cut the pizza into parts.
- Pick up the biggest part.
- Bite into the pizza.
- Lick your lips!

page 3

How to Use a Telephone
1. Read 2. Cut 3. Paste in order

- Pick up the telephone.
- Call the number you want.
- Talk to your friend.
- Hang up the telephone.

page 5

How to Feed the Cat
1. Read 2. Cut 3. Paste in order

- Get a can of cat food and a dish.
- Take the lid off the can.
- Put the cat food in the dish.
- Call your cat.

page 7

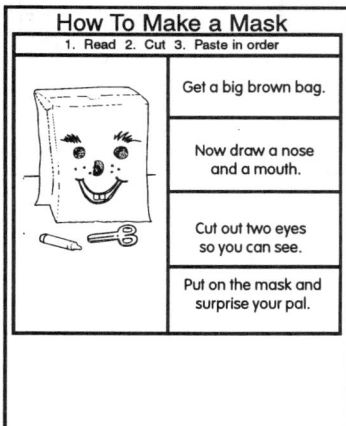

How To Make a Mask
1. Read 2. Cut 3. Paste in order

- Get a big brown bag.
- Now draw a nose and a mouth.
- Cut out two eyes so you can see.
- Put on the mask and surprise your pal.

page 9

How to Put on a Jacket
1. Read 2. Cut 3. Paste in order

- It is a cold day. Get your jacket.
- Put your arms in the sleeves.
- Zip up your jacket
- Now you can go out to play.

page 11

How to Eat a Cookie
1. Read 2. Cut 3. Paste in order

- Take two cookies out of the box.
- Take your cookies outside and sit on the back step.
- Take big bites and eat them up.
- Lick the last bits off your fingers.

page 13

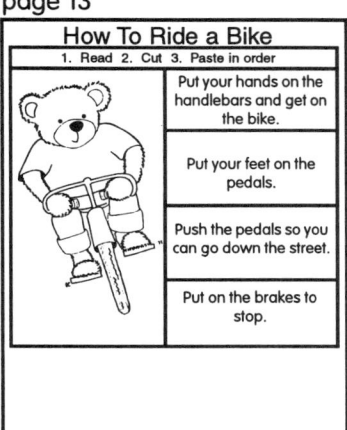

How To Ride a Bike
1. Read 2. Cut 3. Paste in order

- Put your hands on the handlebars and get on the bike.
- Put your feet on the pedals.
- Push the pedals so you can go down the street.
- Put on the brakes to stop.

page 15

How to Make an Ice Cream Cone
1. Read 2. Cut 3. Paste in order

- First get a scoop and a cone.
- Then get the ice cream from the freezer.
- Take a big scoop of ice cream and put it on the cone.
- Take a big lick and gobble it down.

page 17

How to clean Your Dog
1. Read 2. Cut 3. Paste in order

- Fill your tub with water and get a big towel.
- Now catch your dog.
- Put him in the water.
- Rub the suds all over your dog.
- Wash the suds off the dog.
- Dry him with the big towel and let him go.

page 19

How To Catch a Tadpole
1. Read 2. Cut 3. Paste in order

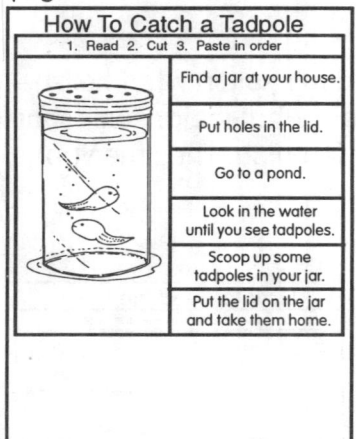

Find a jar at your house.

Put holes in the lid.

Go to a pond.

Look in the water until you see tadpoles.

Scoop up some tadpoles in your jar.

Put the lid on the jar and take them home.

page 21

How to Pick an Apple
1. Read 2. Cut 3. Paste in order

Get a bag and a ladder.

Put the ladder by the tree.

Go up the ladder.

Pick the apples and put them in the bag.

Go down the ladder.

Take the bag of apples in the house.

page 23

How to Wrap a Gift
1. Read 2. Cut 3. Paste in order

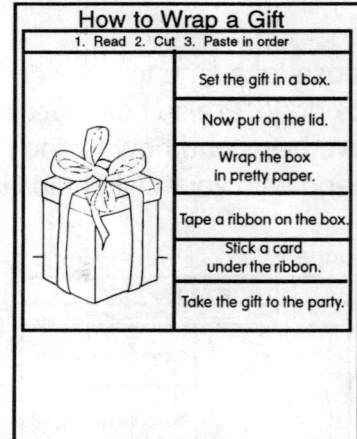

Set the gift in a box.

Now put on the lid.

Wrap the box in pretty paper.

Tape a ribbon on the box.

Stick a card under the ribbon.

Take the gift to the party.

page 25

How To Take a Bath
1. Read 2. Cut 3. Paste in order

Fill the tub with water.

Add bubble bath.

Get into the tub.

Wash with soap and a rag.

Get out of the tub and dry off.

Get dressed.

page 27

How to Make a Sandwich
1. Read 2. Cut 3. Paste in order

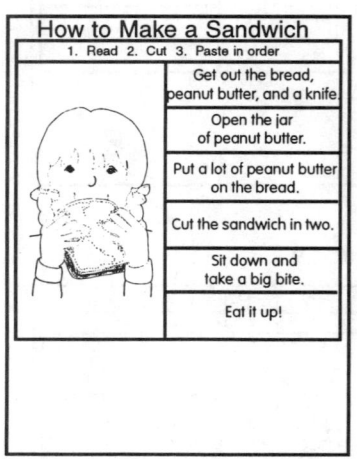

Get out the bread, peanut butter, and a knife.

Open the jar of peanut butter.

Put a lot of peanut butter on the bread.

Cut the sandwich in two.

Sit down and take a big bite.

Eat it up!

page 29

How to Plant a Seed
1. Read 2. Cut 3. Paste in order

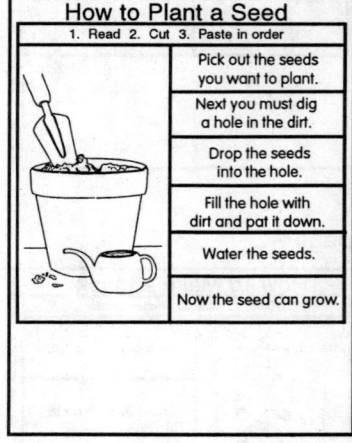

Pick out the seeds you want to plant.

Next you must dig a hole in the dirt.

Drop the seeds into the hole.

Fill the hole with dirt and pat it down.

Water the seeds.

Now the seed can grow.